BRADWELL'S IMA

Norfolk

BRADWELL
BOOKS

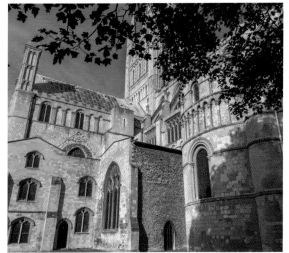

A TASTE OF NORFOLK

KING'S LYNN · BRANCASTER · NORWICH · CLEY-NEXT-THE-SEA · CROMER

Introduction

Welcome to Bradwell's Images of Norfolk – a lovingly prepared collection of photographs that cannot fail to whet your appetite to explore the region for yourself, and we hope will act as a constant reminder of the sheer beauty of Norfolk.

Photographers Susan and Andrew Caffrey have a deep passion for Norfolk and its delightful landscape, a passion that is clearly reflected in each of these unique and stunning images. The book is divided into thirteen distinct areas, each with a short introductory paragraph outlining its main features; however, we think the photographs really speak for themselves.

Enjoy!

Norwich Cathedral

Norwich

The Cow Tower - an artillery tower built in 1398

A modern city with medieval charm, Norwich has plenty to offer. The city centre is easily explored on foot. Wander the cobbled streets and find historic buildings, museums, theatres and ancient pubs. The Norman cathedral is considered one of England's grandest. Norwich also boasts the largest daily outdoor market in the country.

Pull's Ferry - a medieval watergate on the river Wensum

Norwich Castle

St. James Mill 1836

The river Wensum

Historic Elm Hill

All Saints Church

Weybourne

Surrounded by fields, woodland and heathland, Weybourne is excellent for exploring the Norfolk countryside. Walk around this charming little village to see Augustinian remains and typical brick and flint cottages, dating from the 17th century. The pebble beach is a favourite spot for sea-fishing and birdwatching.

Priory Ruins

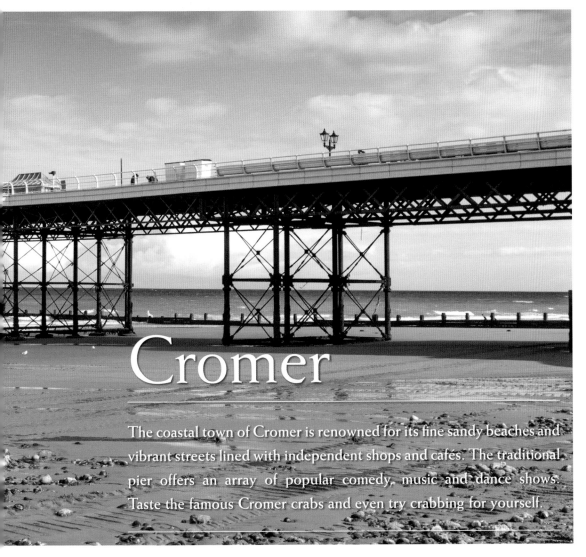

Cromer

The coastal town of Cromer is renowned for its fine sandy beaches and vibrant streets lined with independent shops and cafés. The traditional pier offers an array of popular comedy, music and dance shows. Taste the famous Cromer crabs and even try crabbing for yourself.

Wells NEXT THE SEA

The historic seaside resort of Wells-Next-The-Sea lies on the north Norfolk coast. Its sandy beach, bordered by pine woodland, is a wonderful spot for walking and paddling. Wander down old Staithe Street and find quaint shops, cafes and galleries. The tree-lined Georgian square offers quiet pubs and excellent food.

Happisburgh

Though slowly being eroded by the sea, Happisburgh remains a much-loved tourist stop for its pretty village lanes and golden sands. Take a tour of the iconic lighthouse for an interesting history of the coastline and stunning views from the top.

900 year old Wymondham Abbey

Wymondham

The delightful market town of Wymondham is home to a thriving arts scene and a rich history. In the vibrant town centre, visitors can discover unique shops and museums, sample delicious local produce, and admire the brooding towers of Wymondham Abbey. The annual music festival is a summer highlight.

The Market Cross, built in 1617

Hunstanton's most famous feature is its cliffs, consisting of distinctive layers of red chalk, white chalk and brown sandstone (also known as Carrstone).

Hunstanton

The only west-facing resort on the east coast, Hunstanton is famed for its splendid sunsets. Full of Victorian charm, the town offers plenty of family activities, several gardens, and a land train by which to see the sights. The quieter Old Hunstanton, with its cosy cottages and traditional pubs, is a short walk away.

Brancaster

Brancaster Estate on the north Norfolk coast is an Area of Outstanding Natural Beauty. Wander the Norfolk Coast Path and discover the area's famed scenery and wildlife, and even a Roman fort. Stop by Brancaster Staithe, a working fishing village, to try some first-class shellfish from the residents' stalls.

Mundesley

Small but beautiful, Mundesley offers fresh sea air and a break from the crowds. The sandy beach is thought to be one of the best in Norfolk, and the nearby coast path is perfect for walks. A must-see in the village is the maritime museum, possibly the smallest in England.

Cley NEXT THE SEA

The scenic village of Cley-Next-The-Sea is known for its stunning 18th century windmill, and streets scattered with tea shops and country pubs. Walks may be taken on the nearby Norfolk Coastal Path, from gentle strolls to more challenging routes. The Cley Marshes Nature Reserve is a world-class birdwatching site.

Hunsett Mill on the river Ant, 1 mile north of Barton Broad

Barton Turf

Barton Turf is a peaceful village of pretty cottages and green spaces, the nearest shop a twenty-minute walk away. The staithe and boatyard give access to Barton Broad, the second largest of the Norfolk Broads, home to a dazzling range of birds, fish and otters.

Upton

Along the river Bure lies Upton, a secluded village of narrow lanes and thatched barns. Hanging Hill, a majestic avenue of trees to the north-west, makes for a pleasant walk. Visit Upton Broad and Marshes nature reserve to see some of Norfolk's rarest wildlife, including an impressive array of dragonflies.

Thurne

Thurne shares its name with the river it sits upon, and many visitors arrive here by boat. For some of the best country views, walk up the hill beside the moorings and watch the boats go by. At the top, you'll also find the historic Thurne drainage mill, a favourite attraction.

A TASTE OF NORFOLK

CLEY-NEXT-THE-SEA • UPTON • HORNING